I0491109

SELF
MOTIVATION

How to Get Motivated, Stay Motivated
and Live Motivated!

Dr. Marybeth Crane

www.fitfiftyandfabulous.com

Copyright

© Copyright 2020 - All rights reserved.

It is not legal to reproduce, duplicate, or transmit any part of this document in either electronic means or printed format. Recording of this publication is strictly prohibited, and any storage of this document is not allowed unless with written permission from the publisher except for the use of brief quotations in a book review.

Table of Contents

Foreword:

How to use this book

In preparation:

Buy yourself a beautiful journal and pen. Alternatively, create a special folder on your computer where you will do the journal work suggested.

The book is made up of three different elements:

Information and theory. This is the part you'll need to read.

Journal work. This offers you an opportunity to learn and reflect (the reflection part is an important part of the work).

Practice. Exercises for you to do that will consolidate your learning and help bring about change (the action part of your work).

How can I get the most out of this book?

This book is written in a way that you can choose the best route for you:

Either work through the book from beginning to end. This will give you a complete understanding of all aspects of self-motivation.

Or, pick the chapters where you believe you're having difficulty and work through those first. The book is written in a way that each chapter is an entity on its own. It doesn't require the previous chapter in order to be understood.

On that note: when you work on a chapter, complete the work from the beginning to the end. This is especially true of the journal work. When you get to a journal exercise, do it right away before reading the rest of the chapter. This is because some exercises work better when you do them fresh, before reading the theory behind it. To give yourself the best chance of success, do the journal exercises as you come across them.

As with many things in life, the theory is useful. Real change only comes about when you take action. This includes not only physical action, like making a telephone call, but includes mind action like changing your thought patterns and beliefs.

Mindset changes are possible because you can consciously focus your mind on something specific. For instance, if I suggest that you spend two minutes listing the things you are grateful for in life, you'll find that you are quite capable of doing this. Many of your beliefs are unconscious, but once you become aware of them (through journaling or other exercises) you can consciously let go of that belief and replace it with a more affirming belief — my understanding of action includes this kind of practice and exercise.

Taking action is the most essential consideration to changing your motivation levels. The first action you are going to take is to pick up this book (or download it) and decide how to work with it. Secondly, you will begin reading. Yes, the action gets things moving – and your journey has begun.

Take on all the journal work – this is an important part of the journey of discovery for you. Complete all the exercises as this is part of creating change. Small changes every day make for a lifetime of success. Commit to working though this book. Take your time (don't even try to do it all at once!). If you read the whole book and try to implement all of the changes, you'll lose motivation and be back at square one. That would be like trying to drink fro a firehose!

Try spending a whole week on a chapter — get those changes under your belt before you embark on something new. You may find one or two chapters make all the difference for you. You can end each day flipping though all the key ideas to make the knowledge part of you. Embrace the change. Working through the book means that, in time, you'll shift your motivation levels.

Introduction:

 Let's face it. We are all intrinsically lazy! We have all experienced the frustration of knowing we should be getting up and working on something worthwhile but find ourselves not feeling like doing anything. As the days have gone by with the uncompleted task becoming more and more urgent, the conflict inside has grown until we finally were forced to get up and get to work. And then it's a rush and you feel you can't do justice to the task. At those times you ask yourself: "Why couldn't I just motivate myself to do this long ago??".

Perhaps you've asked yourself many times: "How can I motivate myself?". You may have tried some techniques for a few weeks, but soon found yourself back where you started. Demotivated and frustrated.

Motivation is not necessarily defined as the emotional desire which results in the action. Enthusiasm for a task is often lacking, even though we know it essential. One may say you are motivated to work on a project. Still, if you do not work on it, then you were not sufficiently motivated. There may be times when you have no emotional desire to work, but you motivate yourself to do it anyway. That is when your will simply overrides your emotions and moves your body into action, regardless of your feelings.

Reasons for lack of motivation.

There are many reasons you may lack motivation. The most common ones are:

- Low self-esteem
- Lack of purpose and direction
- Bad health
- Depression and anxiety
- Addiction

This book is based on the premise that you're a reasonably self-regulating person and that you have the ability to take some steps forwards. Now is a good time to ask: "Can I help myself with the help of this book?" Or, "Do I need to see a professional?" I am not a mental health professional. This book will NOT cure depression or stop addictions but boost your motivation. Seek professional help if you feel out of control of your environment.

Consequences of lack of motivation

Lacking motivation can have devastating effects in your life. As you read on, you'll discover that you DON'T have to be motivated to achieve BUT it helps! Most of us suffer from the consequences of being unmotivated in many different ways:

- You struggle to get things done.
- You feel like you can do more with your life, but you don't know how.
- Your heart sinks when you look at your to-do list.
- You sometimes dread getting up to face the day.
- You enter a vicious cycle – the more unmotivated you feel, the less work you do and the worse you feel.
- You feel dissatisfied with yourself and your life.

If you feel like this every now and again – and everyone does at some point – that's okay. When you feel this way every day for most of the day, your happiness levels plummet. The wonderful news is that you can change. Starting right now!

Can motivation be negative?

Yes! A drug addict is highly motivated to get his next fix. A criminal is motivated to surprise his next victim or plan his next heist. The question is not how to get motivated but rather, what to do with it.

Self-motivation is the ability to motivate oneself to do what needs to be done regardless of how one feels. The techniques I will share with you will be ones that help you to choose to "do" when you would rather want to "sit" (or sleep).

This ebook will empower you to get-up-and-go when your "get-up-and-go" has gone up and went. You will learn how to motivate yourself to achieve anything in life.

Let get started.

Chapter 1: What is Motivation?

There are as many definitions for motivation as there are lights in the city. Most people have a pretty good understanding of it.

Motivation is:

- A general desire to do something.
- A willingness to act.
- An inner power that pushes you to action.
- An inner energy needed to accomplish something.
- A desire to achieve a goal.

The best description? Motivation is the inner driving force that gets you going. It's usually seen in a positive light – when you feel motivated, you feel good. Unmotivated, you feel bad.

Being motivated does not mean YOU are good or bad. In the United State, where we have a high crime rate, you will find that the criminal mind is highly motivated. A criminal sets a goal to rob a house and has the inner energy and motivation to reach that goal.

Motivation is part of your human conditioning and it is possible to affect your motivation levels. This is good news, because it means you can empower yourself to achieve your dreams. In this book, you'll learn and practice different ways to up your motivation levels. The more you practice, the better you will get!

One of the quickest and easiest ways to get motivated is to socialize with achievers and people with similar interests or goals. You really are the average of the five people you hang out with the most! Choose wisely! Drive and positive attitudes are contagious. Mix with people who are negative and miserable and it won't be long before you feel the same. You do have the power to choose with whom you socialize – use that power!

Be grateful when you feel motivated. Be even more grateful when you learn how to change from an unresourceful, unmotivated state to an energetic, motivated state. Now you hold the key to success.

The Benefits of Being Self Motivated

Taking responsibility for your own success is the best and only shortcut to success. Therefore, you should know that you are who you want to be and the limit is just within your definition. So what does this mean? It means that individuals need to be self-motivated when pursuing a destiny in their life. If you want to change the path of your future, get rid of a bad habit or improve the way you work. You definitely can gain a lot by practicing self-motivation exercises and getting motivated is what drives you to conquer all your goals and all your dreams. Sometimes though, stresses of day to day life can overwhelm and completely drain us. These day to day pressures can take away our energy and sometimes cause us to lose site of what we were originally after. If you practice some motivational exercises, it would help bring you back to your focus and reshape your life.

The inspiration to wake up every morning and do what you are supposed to be doing should come from yourself, and not forced on you by someone else. It is intrinsic, not extrinsic. Everyone knows what they want and therefore you only can drive yourself to success. Here are some of the advantages of having intrinsic motivation.

1. You Will Not Find Any Possible Barriers

When a person is self-motivated, there is nothing like impossible since the person will work on anything that looks like a barrier. They believe they will eventually make it to the other side. On the contrary, when the force is coming from someone else or an external force, it is very easy to give up and not achieve your goal. The first driving force is usually from an external source, and therefore you just work under supervision. When this person or source of power is not present, you just give up when you are faced with a barrier. This is not the right way to get to the destination; it sets you up for failure. Therefore, individuals should learn to be intrinsically self-motivated so as to hit their targets easily.

2. You Value the Goal and So You Are Going for It

People will have intrinsic driving force when they value the goal. When you know what exactly what you want, you will ultimately go for the goal, and this is because it impacts your life directly. In short, the motivation is based on the satisfaction offered by the goal that you have set. On the contrary, when the goal benefits other parties, (because you see it that way) then it becomes very hard to keep going.

Often in a workplace the staff feels there is no need to burn the midnight oil, because the job you are doing is benefitting someone else, and your salary is just fixed. You have no motivation to go the extra mile. This is the reason why some companies pay sales staff based on commission so that they work harder or more efficiently, motivated by the extra money.

3. You Will Leave No Stone Unturned

Think of the miners, they will literally dig down the furrow even after exhausting the precious stone that was on the site. When they leave that site, don't be surprised when others come to scope anything that might be left there — when a person's inspiration is coming from the inside, this is usually the case. Therefore, you will make sure that you have done all the tasks just to achieve the goal that is in front of you. On the contrary, if you are not motivated, you will just be waiting for the time to pass so as to leave the office no matter how much work is on your desk.

Why Is Keeping Yourself Motivated Such Hard Work?

We all live in a crazy busy world surrounded by so many distractions. It makes it easy for us to get sidetracked and lose sight of what is important to us. We lose sight of what we want and what we should be doing. If there are a lot of distractions that keep you from doing what you need to be doing, then you need to make some changes.

Being motivated means that you are aligned with your goals and values. You are clear on what is important to you and why it is important to you. This helps in maintaining discipline and focus. In order to do this successfully, take the time to determine those values and prioritize the ones that are most important to you.

Keeping yourself motivated means that you have a clear vision of how you and your life will be different once you achieve your goals. More importantly, you use the visualization to generate the powerful feelings associated with successfully achieving the goal. Developing this important skill will allow you to see yourself implementing those important action steps that you need to take in order to achieve your goal.

Rehearsing, preparation, breaking things down into smaller more manageable steps; becoming more organized, determining what is urgent and non-urgent, and what will become urgent if not addressed, will go a long way towards reducing distraction and embracing the hard work that is needed to get you where you want to go. Using the power of visualization with any one of these steps will keep you focused and enhance your self- motivation.

Keeping yourself motivated requires a high level of self-discipline, self-honesty and self-monitoring to deal with the distractions that can get in your way. In monitoring your thoughts, actions and behaviors you accept the fact that you alone are accountable and responsible for the outcome of your success.

Motivated people find a way! They are able to do what needs to be done, without influence from other situations or people. They do not give up when challenged, as they are able to rely on their own strength, reason, and resilience. Although you can certainly benefit from encouragement and support, at the end of the day your achievement of success will come down to your inner abilities. To be self-motivated means that there is no outside force or person pushing you to become what you want to be. The locus of control is within you and not based on others.

Motivation Myths:

Myth 1: I have to be motivated before I start working

Not true! Almost every day of your life you do things you don't really feel like doing. Think of days when you haven't felt like going to work, but you still did.

"I just don't feel like it." When you believe this statement, you put off doing tasks because you don't feel like you're motivated – even though you are quite capable of doing the task.

Myth 2: My boss/company/spouse/another should motivate me

Not true! Take responsibility for motivating yourself. Saying that it's the company's fault that they aren't motivating you is disempowering (for you). You're NOT likely to get far in life if you believe this. Is your success in life really that dependant on others? Be accountable and responsible for your own success, your own motivation and your own choices.

Myth 3: Fear is a good motivator

Not entirely true! Fear certainly does motivate and can get results. However, it's not always sustainable. And, when fear loses its power, you may start floundering. Fear motivation often causes cyclical successes. For example, let's say you have a fear of being fat and ugly. You wake up, look in the mirror and you say to yourself, "That's it, you look dreadful. All that weight is revolting. If you carry on like this you will be obese and no-one will want to be with you."

Your fear motivates you to do something. You decide to join a weight-loss group and you're highly motivated. The weight starts dropping slowly and steadily. One day you look in the mirror and you say, "You're looking great! Look how good those clothes look on you – time to celebrate!" And off you go to a celebratory meal with your friends.

You have a little extra over the weekend. You "need" a glass of wine after a hard day at work. Slowly but surely the weight comes back. What happened? The moment you looked in the mirror and decided you were fine, the fear of being fat was not there – and your motivation to diet was GONE. Without the motivation, there's not much incentive to diet. So you start putting on weight until one day you look in the mirror and say "That's it, you look dreadful. All that weight is revolting. If you carry on like this you will be obese and no-one will want to be with you...."

And so the rollercoaster starts – motivated by fear, you spring into action. Fear goes away, you lose motivation. Fear comes back, and you're back at work, etc., etc. Fear may motivate but it's not the best way to create success in your life.

Myth 4: I am not motivated

Not true! (Unless you are severely clinically depressed.) Everyone is motivated about something – even if it's to lie in bed on a Sunday morning. Ever "desperately" wanted that glass of wine at the end of the day? That's motivation. You believe you aren't motivated when you don't want to do the things that you feel you SHOULD be doing. When you feel like doing something that you believe you SHOULD be doing then you say you're motivated.

Motivation is merely a strong desire to do something (whether you feel you should or should not). You ARE experiencing that feeling on a regular basis.

Myth 5: Motivation is only for work tasks

Not true! People are motivated to do all sorts of different things: play sport, build strong relationships, to be more spiritual, to sleep on the couch on a Sunday afternoon, to climb mountains and swim in freezing rivers..... The list is endless. Motivation is merely a strong desire to do something.

Myth 6: Giving rewards motivates people

Not entirely true! Like fear, it can result in getting people to do things that they may not really want to do. This way of motivating is called extrinsic motivation.

The problem with this method of motivating people is that they'll focus on getting the task done as quickly and effortlessly as possible because their eye is on the reward and not on the task. They're motivated to get the reward. They're not motivated to do the task well – simply to get it finished.

For example, when I'm filing papers (which is something I hate doing), I set a timer for half an hour. I file furiously, and when the half hour is done, I sit down with a nice cup of coffee and do something that I enjoy (like writing this book). The problem is that sometimes I file documents in the wrong place because all I want is to get it over with and have my coffee. I'm motivated to clear my desk, but not necessarily motivated to file correctly. I don't intend changing my way of getting the filing done because most of the time this method works for me (nobody else looks at my files anyway). However, this may not be a useful method to motivate myself when I am teaching someone. "Let's get this done as quickly as possible so that I can go shopping" would not add that much value to my teaching practice!

Journal work

Think about the way you run your life. Write down all your extrinsic motivators – as many as you can. What motivates you to keep healthy? What motivates you to see your family and friends? What motivates you to go to work? What motivates you to watch TV for hours? What motivates you to spend hours on social media? Be HONEST! For example:

When I avoid conflict it's because I fear losing my job.

When I avoid doing a report I don't understand it's because I don't want my boss to know that I can't do it.

When I reach for that glass of wine I tell myself it's because I had a long week and deserve it. What I really want is to forget all my troubles.

Motivation Truths:

Truth 1: Motivation is a luxury – you don't have to have it!

So true! A luxury is desirable but not essential – and, it's often something that's hard to get. So too with motivation! If you have a job to do and you're highly motivated – that's wonderful – enjoy it. However, we are all completely capable of doing something we don't feel like doing — we are capable of working even when we're unmotivated and most people have experienced that feeling. If you're not feeling motivated, acknowledge your attitude AND do it anyway.

Truth 2: Motivation is catchy

So true! Think back to a time when you were extremely motivated to do something. How high were your enthusiasm levels? Probably quite high... Motivation and enthusiasm seem to go hand in hand. In fact, one of the definitions in the dictionary for motivation is enthusiasm. And, enthusiasm is highly contagious. Therefore, we can also deduce that motivation is catchy.

If you're working on a project with someone who is highly motivated and enthusiastic, there's a strong possibility that you'll begin feeling the same way. So if you're concerned that you're unmotivated about a task, start faking the enthusiasm until it becomes real – and the motivation will follow. "Fake it until you make it!"

Truth 3: You're motivated by the consequences of your work

So true! If you are feeling unmotivated about a task, think about the outcomes of it. If the outcome inspires you in some way (hopefully it does, otherwise why are you doing it?), then visualize that outcome using all your senses. Run this movie through your head often to help with your motivation levels.

Truth 4: Start the work, motivation will follow

So true! I experienced this over and over again while writing this book. Often I did not feel like sitting down and writing. So I'd say to myself, "I don't feel like this, and I'll write anyway." If I felt bad, I'd promise myself that if, after 20 minutes; if I still did not feel like it, I could stop — that never happened. Once I got going, my motivation levels rose, and then I did not want to stop.

This is also true when starting a running program. You often don't want to start because you fear it will hurt or be too difficult. What's impressive is that if you force yourself to start, after the first few minutes, you don't want to stop! So get going, even if you don't feel like it – motivation will sneak in while you're working.

Truth 5: Motivation is a habit

So true! Humans often develop habitual ways of being in the world. If you've developed an attitude where you see hard work as negative and unpleasant, you'll mostly feel unmotivated. If you focus on the hard work instead of the outcome of the hard work, you will feel unmotivated. If you say to yourself how awful it is and how much you hate it, you're unlikely to feel motivated. Fortunately, the opposite is also true. If you focus on the outcomes of any project and your attitude towards work is healthy, you're likely to feel motivated about most things in your life. Attitude is a habit. Focus is a habit. Motivation is a habit.

Journal work

Explore your habitual way of being in the world.

What are your common thoughts?

In what areas do you display a healthy attitude and where in your life does your attitude not add value?

Describe your enthusiasm levels for different aspects of your life.

Where do you need to make changes?

Chapter 2: Your Motivators

What motivates you? This is a question asked by many people and companies. The answer is quite simple: you are driven by what you value. Your motivators are aligned with your value system. Of course it's not always that simple to identify your highest values but it's not that difficult either. It simply means you need to do a bit of detective work!

Journal work

Write a list of all the values that you can think of. Aim for about 40 to 50. These are not necessarily your values but rather any values you know of. For example:

Honesty.
Reliability.
Support.
Belonging.

There are three important corners to the motivation triangle:

Your resources. This applies to your skills, abilities, knowledge, people and tools available to help you and your attitude and beliefs.

Your goal.

Your personal values.

Most people simply focus on the goal and their resources. An important link, often ignored, is the congruency between the goal and your personal values. A person who puts high value on honesty and integrity is unlikely to achieve a goal of robbing a bank. Your goal must encompass your personal values for your motivation levels to be high. Obviously, all your resources must be available for you to be motivated and to reach your goals. We know this to be true: if you're assigned to a job for which you are totally incompetent, you're unlikely to feel motivated about the job.

Identify your personal values. This is essential if you want to be successful. Understanding personal values is an outcome of self-learning and self-reflection.

For example: Let's say James makes lots of money. It's easy to look at that picture and say that James is motivated by material things. However, he may be driven by the need for security or the need to be the best. Or, simply to be successful. A value detective might take a closer look at James' home and office. What's he got on the walls and which is important to him? Certificates and diplomas may mean he values success and acknowledgement. Beautiful paintings may mean he appreciates creativity and aesthetics. Paintings of scenery and the outdoors could indicate that he enjoys being in nature or being at peace. All of these give us a clearer picture of James' personal values. It's these personal values that drive him to do what he does. The money may merely be an outcome of his work and may not necessarily reflect these values. Bear this in mind when you look for signs of your own personal value system.

Another aspect to consider is your spending habits. When you have spare cash – what do you spend it on? Music could mean that relaxation or creativity is important to you. Buying clothes could indicate that grooming is meaningful or, being attractive, is vital to you. These are just examples and each scenario will be different for each person. Only you will know which underlying values are important to you in each case.

The way you live your life provides good clues as to what you value. If you say your children are important to you, yet you spend very little time with them. Acknowledge that perhaps your career aspirations may give you more meaning. Look at the kinds of holidays you take and the way you spend your leisure time. All of this gives you clues about your personal values.

Journal work

Answer this question:

What must I have in my life in order to be fulfilled?

Write whatever comes into your mind and spend at least 30 minutes on it. Allow yourself to get into the flow of your answer and don't stop until you feel it's complete.

Be careful when identifying your values: make sure you are not picking values that are socially acceptable but not yours. Maybe integrity is preached about regularly in your church, but this may not mean it's a top value of yours. It may still be important to you but perhaps not one of your top three. Watch your feelings carefully – you will feel congruent when you list true values – and perhaps a little uncomfortable when you list adopted, socially-accepted values.

Have a look at your weekly activities. What does this tell you about your values? If you play a lot of sport, what's driving you? Do you have a need to look good? Does the need to achieve drive you? Or, is your need to be healthy your main motivator? You only ever do something when you find personal value in doing it. You can determine this by asking yourself what's really important to you about doing sport, as an example.

Journal work

Take some time to do this exercise. Take the values that you wrote down in the previous journal exercise and add them to the list below. Add any other values that come up as you do this. You may give the values different names. You may combine values if you feel they describe the same sentiment. You may add values if you feel there is something important missing. Close your journal and take a few days to think.

Support (to/from family).
Quality relationships.
Fulfilment.
Growth.
Achievement.

Contribution.
Belonging.
Responsibility.
Connection to God.
Appreciation.
Respect.
Making a difference.
Development.
Commitment.
Quality of work.
Sharing Joy.
Overall structure.
Comfort.
Creativity.
Transformation.
Self worth.
Freedom.
Connection with people.
Open mindedness.
Learning.
Having a different perspective.
Unlocking potential.
Communication.
Empowering others.
Honesty.
Flexibility.
Ability to choose.

Once you've identified your highest values, you can use them to motivate yourself. If quality relationships and appreciation are high on your value system, how can your work help you align with these values? Nurturing good quality relationships at work will allow you to persuade people to support your point of view at times when you need support to achieve something. Spending time appreciating your staff, colleagues and bosses allows you to build relationships and align with both values – this will lead to harmony in the workplace which, in turn, allows for greater success.

Journal work

Take some time to do this exercise. Look at the list of values that you have created. Choose your 12 most important values from the list. Take your time and think it through. When you find yourself struggling to choose between two values, look at what your life demonstrates as most important to you. Once you have completed your list of 12 values, take a break.

Come back to the exercise and work with your 12 highest values. Write down your values in list format numbered one to 12. For example, your list could look something like this:

Freedom.
Learning.
Belonging.
Sharing.
Success.
Growth.
Creativity.
Aesthetics.
Self worth.
Connection to God.
Honesty.
Contribution.

If possible, get a friend or spouse to help you with the rest of this exercise. Go through each value one at a time comparing it with every other one. Each time you compare two values, place a tick next to the one that is most important to you.

To elaborate:

Compare value 1 and value 2, ticking the most important.
Compare value 1 and value 3, ticking the most important.
Compare value 1 and value 4, etc. all the way up to 1 and 12.
Go on to value 2.

Compare value 2 and value 3, ticking the most important.
Compare value 2 and value 4, ticking the most important.
Compare value 2 and value 5, etc. all the way up to 2 and 12.
Go on to value 3.
Compare value 3 and value 4, ticking the most important.
Compare value 3 and value 5, ticking the most important.
Compare value 3 and value 6, etc. all the way up to 3 and 12.
Go on to value 4.
Compare value 4 and value 5, ticking the most important.
Compare value 4 and value 6, ticking the most important.
Compare value 4 and value 7, etc. all the way up to 4 and 12.
Continue doing the same throughout....

When you are done, count the ticks to determine your most important values. Do not be stressed if you are surprised by the outcome. This often happens!

How do you know if what you're doing is aligned with your values? Simply take note of your feelings. Uncomfortable feelings are a good indicator that you're doing something that compromises your values. Feeling focused, connected and calm often indicates that what you're doing is aligned with your values. More detective work required!

Journal work

Consider the society in which you operate. Write down 20 to 30 values of your society. Then, consider your value system. Which of your values align with those of your community? Which ones don't? What outcomes do you experience that arise from the difference in your value systems?

Think back to the last time you were really angry? What specifically caused that anger? Think through your answer as it often points to a value of yours. For example: "I was so angry because he treated her with disrespect!" This probably points to values of respect or self-worth amongst others. Or, "I was so angry that he did not consult me on the matter." This may point to the values of respect, acknowledgement, contribution or self-worth. Or, "I was so angry when he humiliated me in public," could point to values of self-worth, integrity or appreciation. You'll know best what the relevant values are for you. When your anger button is pushed it's often because, your value system is being compromised.

Practice:

Pay attention to your feelings daily. Make a note of moments when you're feeling congruent and authentic. What was going on right then? What was being honoured in the moment that allowed you to feel like this?

Make a note of moments you feel angry, irritated or even uncomfortable and explore that situation? What values were being suppressed? What important beliefs were being compromised?

Read your answers carefully and write down the values that are important to you. Keep a record of your values as you discover them.

Knowing your values means that you can learn to motivate yourself. Every time you do something it's because you find personal value in doing it — usually this is unconscious. Now you have the opportunity to make it more conscious.

Let's say you set a goal to complete an advanced degree. You've done some work and you've discovered your highest values are respect, adventure and friendship. How will having your degree meet your value of respect? That's relatively simple: completing your degree means that you can respect yourself for achieving something. You'll also gain respect from your family, friends and work colleagues.

How will completing your advanced degree meet your value of adventure? Perhaps you can see your studies as an adventure. You'll be learning something new, meeting new people and discovering things about yourself that were not there before. Perhaps completing your degree will translate into greater financial rewards in time – this will give you the ability to afford adventure holidays. You could also treat yourself to mini-adventures when you achieve smaller milestones in your studies. You could arrange to go hiking (or whatever means adventure to you – learn to tango or surf?) after you have completed ten assignments. What about the value of friendship? Decide to get into a study group. Go to all your tutorials. Form a peer group where you chat on Skype once a week to discuss problems you're experiencing with the studies. All these are opportunities to make new friends. You may find those bonds formed during studying last a lifetime.

Once you realise that getting the advanced degree gives you congruence with your top values, it will be much easier to study. Remind yourself of the ways it is enriching your life by meeting your values. Include these images in your visualisation when you wake in the mornings. Studying for a degree will make more sense to you now.

Journal work

How can you use the knowledge of your values to motivate yourself to achieve your goals? In what ways are you compromising your values by NOT taking action?

Write down a big goal of yours. Write down two or three ways that achieving that goal will be congruent with your top five values. What resources (internal and external) do you need in order to achieve your goal? Are all of these at your disposal? What can be done to get all of these resources on board?

Working with your value system is a life-long study. This is because values can change as you grow and mature. Some core values will stay the same; others may change as you mature. For instance, a person in their twenties may value success and integrity. By the time they are in their fifties, they may value giving back to society over and above success at work, but integrity will probably still rank highly.

Keeping in mind that every person has a different set of values, the table below indicates the general values for different age groups that exist today. The different values arise from the different experiences that each generation has gone through.

Age group

Values
Over 55
Privacy, hard work, trust, formality, authority, order, possessions

35–55
Competition, change, hard work, success, body language, teamwork, anti-rules and -regulations, fighting for a cause

25-35
Entrepreneurial spirit, independence, creativity, information, feedback, flexibility, quality of life

0-25
Positive reinforcement, autonomy, positive attitudes, diversity, money, technology

It may seem like a lot of work to discover your values but it's worth it. There are numerous benefits associated with knowing your unique value system. It is much easier to make decisions when you can weigh up the outcomes against your values. You will experience a sense of internal alignment and authenticity when you live according to your values. Your life purpose becomes clearer. Stress is reduced when you consciously make choices aligned with your values. Living according to your own value system makes life's challenges seem less overwhelming

If your life choices are generally not in alignment with your values, you will feel apathetic, unmotivated, conflicted and stressed. Motivation comes easily to those who understand their values and make choices accordingly. When you choose a project or goal that is well-aligned with your values, you don't have to worry about how to motivate yourself. Motivation will come naturally.

Journal work

How do your values compare with the table above?

Do they match the age group you are in? How do your values differ?

What does this say about you?

Fear is a distressing emotion caused by anticipation OR awareness of danger. Your ability to experience fear is part of your basic survival mechanism. Fear is the emotion that enables you to recognize danger and you usually react by fleeing from the danger or confronting it. This is known as the fight or flight response. There's also a third possible reaction which is the freeze response. This is where your mind and body slow down and you're unable to react. Fear is completely natural and helps people recognise and respond to dangerous situations and threats.

Fear is a negative and uncomfortable emotion. When fear's present you are unable to feel motivated (a positive and uplifting emotion). Fear saps your energy, whereas motivation creates energy. When you want something and are unable to go after it, it's often because your fear is much stronger than your desire. Have you ever wanted to leave a job or relationship, but fear has held you back? We all experience fear at some time in our lives. Common forms of fear include fear of failure, rejection, loneliness, loss, being powerful, not being powerful etc. The list goes on and on. The biggest issue with fear is that fear often stops you from going out there and getting what you want.

Fear is a feeling. You may invalidate your feelings by thinking, "I shouldn't be feeling scared." Don't do this. Every feeling is real. Acknowledge them and then go ahead and do what you want to do despite the fear. You can pack the fear in your bag and take it with you on your journey. An empowered person may say something like, "I'm terrified of getting up and speaking in public, BUT I'm going to learn how to do it anyway." This statement acknowledges the feeling and decides to go ahead anyway. It's a myth that fears stop you. The reality is that YOU allow this to happen; you choose to remain stuck and blame it on the fear.

Martha Beck distinguishes between clean fear and dirty fear. Clean fear is experienced when you're facing actual danger. Clean fear reminds you not to put your hands in boiling water, or to run in front of a bus. Clean fear is an appropriate fear.

The amazing thing is that your mind and body can't distinguish between clean (real) fear and dirty (imagined) fear. Your brain is an amazing movie-maker: you're able to instantaneously picture large, vibrant scenes accompanied by sounds, smells and textures. Dirty fear ignores the facts (like right now you're perfectly safe) and embellishes your worries in a toxic and dramatic way. Your imagination can put your body into fight, flight or freeze mode, and create physical symptoms like a madly beating heart, shallow breathing and a sense of panic. A dear friend of mine describes how she eventually finds herself deciding what to wear to the funeral when her husband is late coming home. When you believe a fear to be true (even if it's not) your whole body reacts accordingly.

Dirty fear turns you into a victim – you're powerless to do much in the face of an imagined fear. When you feel powerless you become de-motivated. When you feel de-motivated you're unable to take action. The fear you experience is not the problem – it's the fact that YOU allow it to limit you in such an effective way. I define dirty fear as "False Events Appearing Real."

Practice:

Use alarms to do this check every four hours: rate your anxiety levels on a scale of 0 (totally relaxed and peaceful) to 10 (highly stressed and anxious, beating heart, shallow breathing etc). If you answered five or more, then ask yourself whether the issue causing this anxiety is true right now.

Keep a record of your answers for about ten days. What do your answers show you?

Learn to discern the dirty fears from the clean ones. It's not difficult – any moment when you are experiencing anxiety, check if there's true, immediate danger. The majority of the time you'll find there isn't. Also, when you experience clean fear – you'll find that you are totally present and in the moment. When you cross a busy road, your mind is aware as you cross. You won't be wondering what to eat for lunch as you cross the road!

When your mind is busy with dirty fear – you're not completely present. When you're worrying about your partner being unfaithful, or running out of money, or being retrenched, your mind is busy with some future possibility; it's not dealing with the present moment.

Practice

Allocate half an hour each week to indulge your dirty fears. Any other time during the week when you find yourself in dirty fear space, stop immediately, make a note of the fear, and gently tell yourself you'll think about that fear again during your allocated dirty fear time.

Consciously focus your mind on the task at hand. When it's time for your weekly "dirty fear indulgence," look at your list and enjoy spending half an hour imagining the worst possible scenarios.

Now write down three actions you could take to prevent these scenarios and then take them.

Generally speaking, clean fear sends you into immediate action. Dirty fear does not. As your awareness grows and you find certain fears dominate your life – think about what action you can take to reduce the possibility of your dirty fear becoming a reality. For instance, if you worry about your partner being unfaithful, what steps can you take towards building and strengthening your relationship? Take action. If you're worrying about your money situation, what steps can you take to create a more secure financial position? Take action. You'll find the more action you take in the face of your imagined fears, the more those imagined worries diminish.

The less time you spend on dirty, imagined fears, the more motivated you'll feel about your life. The more motivated you feel, the more energy you'll have to expend on actions that create the kind of life you enjoy living.

After all, it's difficult to feel motivated if you're feeling anxious and stressed. Reducing the amount of time you spend in an anxious and distressed state allows you to dedicate more positive energy to living an enjoyable life.

Journal work

Turn to a clean page in your journal and title it: "My Worry Journal." For the next month, every time you find yourself worrying about something, write it down in your journal and then let it go out of your mind by focusing on the present moment and the task at hand. At the end of the month, go through your list and cross off everything that didn't happen.

What have you got left?

Chapter 4: Procrastination

Journal work

Write freely and without restriction for at least half an hour.

Answer this question: "How do I know when to procrastinate?"

This topic is a book in its own right. (Yes, I already wrote that one.) One of the problems with procrastination is that you tend to throw out blanket statements like, "I always procrastinate," which is never 100% accurate. Yet, you label yourself with this 'fact' and you see yourself as a PROCRASTINATOR.

Journal work

If you're a procrastinator answer these questions in your journal:

So I'm a procrastinator. Is that all I am?

How much more am I than just "a procrastinator"?

Write down ten other (affirming!) nouns that describe you. For example, "I'm an inspirer." "I'm a leader." "I'm a problem-solver."

Know that these other nouns also have elements of truth in them, just as "I'm a procrastinator" does. But neither are they absolutely true. Notice the change in feelings when you describe yourself as a procrastinator and then when you describe yourself using an affirmative noun. Where do you feel this in your body? Write down your experiences of the different feelings.

Procrastination is your propensity to decide to do something later that you believe you should be doing now. In reality, you are choosing in that moment the action you will be taking next. Like thinking: "Mmm, I think I'll check my emails quickly instead of writing this chapter on procrastination," and off you go and spend time working on things that are not that important and usually, may not add value to your life.

"You cannot get motivated passively. In fact, motivation is the opposite of procrastination. Motivation is doing something... now! Procrastination is doing nothing... now! Something... Nothing..." - Larry Hendrick

Journal work

Write down 20 sentences in your journal that each begins with "I can't..." For example:

I can't make money.

I can't win with my kids

I can't do the marathon.

There are a few upsides to procrastination. People who procrastinate regularly work extremely well under pressure. This is because you continually put things off, leave things to the last-minute and then work under tight deadlines to get it done. You get good at this! People who procrastinate regularly are capable of doing many things in a short space of time. People who procrastinate regularly are able to focus intensely when needed. Deadlines have their uses – they enable you to complete projects and to work under pressure. If you stopped focusing on the fact that you were a procrastinator, you could say that you work well under pressure. You recognize that you have the ability to focus intensely and that you are able to do much in a short space of time.

Of course, the issue with procrastinating is that you put undue stress on yourself because you tend to leave things to the last minute. This leads you to believe that you only work well under pressure. So if there is no pressure (i.e., the deadline is far away) then you believe you can't work. This is similar to believing that you can't work because you don't feel like it.

Beliefs are powerful! Let's see what happens when you believe something. For example, the belief: "I can't work without pressure." Notice that this is just a thought. Yet you treat it as if it's a 'fact.' A fact is 100% true and is irrefutable. You choose your behavior according to the facts that surround the situation. You can't work unless under pressure becomes an acceptable way of being and you don't challenge this idea. You believe it; you treat it as an irrefutable fact and you live your life according to this principle. Essentially, you give up on yourself. You actually sabotage your success by buying into this fact.

Don't forget this: Every time you do something it's because you find personal value in doing it.

This is a bit strange. What personal value could you possibly find by hanging onto this particular belief as if it were a rule by which to live your life? This is where you have to dig deep. Perhaps you find some bizarre personal value in beating yourself up and putting yourself down. Perhaps the work is uninspiring and procrastinating is your way of protecting yourself from boredom. Perhaps buying into this excuse allows you to live a mediocre life and that's what you believe you deserve. The reality is that holding onto the belief that you can't work without pressure let's you off the hook. The personal value in this case is that you are not accountable – after all, you believe it to be true so there's nothing you can do about it.

Once you realize that you're holding onto such a belief, you can begin to realize how limiting this is for you and how severely it holds you back. Usually just the awareness that you believe this statement allows you to let go of it.

Journal work

Write down a limiting belief that you hold. For example: "I am a procrastinator" OR "I can't work without pressure" OR "I always leave things to the last minute." Then, answer the following questions in your journal:

Is it true?

Is it absolutely 100% true (100% of the time)? How do I know this is absolutely true?

How do I react when I think that thought? Write down some specific examples.

Who would I be without that thought? Describe your life if you never had that thought again.

Write down one or more opposite statements. For example, "I can work without pressure" OR "I can work anytime I choose to." Examine your life and find three situations where this is true. Write down specific examples.

Do NOT stop this exercise until you really get that the opposite is also true but not absolutely true.

 When you focus on procrastinating and calling yourself a procrastinator – you're affecting your motivation levels. When you do procrastinate, you use up energy stressing about what you're not doing. This negative energy affects your psyche. This eats away at your motivation. When you label yourself as a procrastinator, how can you expect to be motivated?

Feeling motivated is about feeling good and ready to take on your challenges. Holding onto limiting beliefs about procrastination erodes away at motivation.
Let go of your procrastination issues and build your motivation levels instead.

Chapter 5: Best Practices

Business defines 'best practice' as a technique or methodology that reliably leads to the desired result. A commitment to using the 'best practices' in any field is a commitment to using all the knowledge and technology at one's disposal to ensure success.

This works well in business. It can also be extremely useful in your personal life. 'Best practices' are the things you do that that allow you to be your very best. For example: exercising regularly gives you energy and keeps you in the emotional state that you need to be in order to work on a goal.

When you think about motivation there are activities that decrease motivation and others that increase motivation. Here are some 'best practices' that could help you to be the best you could be:

Get up early and spend an hour in prayer or meditation, self-reflection and self-development.

Exercise regularly.

Eat healthy five days a week.

Journal to develop self-awareness.

Read to gather new ideas and self-understanding.

Affirm yourself for a few minutes at the end of the day.

Do weekly planning sessions where you can revise goals and set tasks for the week ahead.

Switch off the computer at 7 pm each day and relax with a novel and a cup of decaf coffee or tea in the garden.

Do what needs to be done, even if you don't feel like it.

Create a movie in your head that depicts the big picture for your life and run through it every time you sit behind the wheel of your car.

Batch jobs. For example: spend one hour working on a task, then 20 minutes on emails followed by half an hour returning calls: this allows more efficiency in your day.

There are many more ideas that could be added to the list. Each person is different and unique and will need different 'best practices' that will work in their lives. The point is that small, constructive actions taken on a daily basis will give you a sense of accomplishment. Doing this also creates momentum. Repeated actions form a habit. These daily habits form the foundation for change in the long term. Develop your 'best practices' and live your best life!

Journal work

Write down all the 'best practices' you can think of that would support you in being your best.
Highlight the ones that could increase your motivation levels.

Practice

Pick one 'best practice' – the one that you feel would make the most difference in your life.

Implement this practice and turn it into a habit.

Self Reflection

Self-reflection is essential to your growth and development. All it takes is a few quiet moments, away from the hustle and bustle of life, where you quietly and calmly look at yourself and your life. Ask yourself some useful questions like:

What's not working in my life?
What do I have the power to change?
What's working?
What should I continue doing?
What aspects of my behavior are not adding value to my life?

You may want to do this work in a journal if you find that your thoughts jump all over the place. I certainly find my thoughts are more focused if I write things down. Regular self-reflection followed by taking action gives you a feeling of being empowered and in control of your life.

Part of your self-reflection strategy could be focused on monitoring your motivation levels. It's normal for motivation levels to fluctuate. Through self-reflection you can become aware if you're mostly motivated about your life, or mostly unmotivated. This will give you an idea of where to direct your energies. You can use your motivation levels to guide you to necessary change.

If you have low motivation levels most of the time, this indicates that you must change something about your life. If you do nothing, and carry on the way you are for another ten years, how would that be for you? What needs to happen so that can you feel fulfilled? Do you need to change careers or get help to deal with a bad relationship? Have you been for a medical exam recently? Then, if you don't feel empowered to make the changes you need to make, consider seeing a life coach or psychologist. Remember you are the only one who can help YOU to make a shift. Take the steps needed to sort out your life.

If your motivation levels are okay but could do with a boost, there are lots you can do. Self-reflection is a very good start. Do the following practice and start learning about yourself and how you function. The better you understand yourself, the easier it'll become to shift yourself consciously into higher motivation states.

Journal work

Write in your journal, once a month, about the areas in your life where you're feeling unmotivated. Write down all the details:

How did this situation come about?

Who is involved?

How would I like it to be?

What is my role in creating the situation?

What changes can I make?

What have I learnt from this book that I could apply?

Here's a serious consideration: there will always be aspects of your life that are not working. Don't focus on these issues on a daily basis – this will lead to negativity and unhappiness. Once a month, sit down and reflect on what's not working. Identify what is OUT of your control and what is IN your control. If the 'not working' is about someone else's behaviors, you DON'T have much power over it, and focusing on it incessantly will leave you feeling frustrated, irritated and sometimes depressed.

What you DO have control over is your own thoughts, feelings, attitudes and behaviours towards this person. I get that this is hard to swallow! What you can do and have the power to do is to reflect on your own issues and change something you are doing, saying or thinking. In this way, you can influence the other person's reaction towards you.

Learn to let go of issues that are outside of your control – focusing on these issues causes you undue emotional stress and pain. Focus on being the change that you want in your life. This is where your power lies.

Practice

Do this for a month. At lunch time every day rate your levels of motivation for the past five hours on a scale of 0 to 5:

0 = totally unmotivated

3 = average motivation levels

5 = highly motivated

Each day write brief notes to explain your rate. Plot the rate of your motivation on a graph at the end of every week. After a month, sit back and reflect on your these levels. Have they increased or decreased? Are there any patterns that you notice? How can you use the information that you have learned from this exercise to motivate yourself in the future?

The Right Attitude

What is attitude?

Your attitude is the way in which you respond to your environment.

How is attitude formed?

It's mostly derived from your beliefs about you and the systems in which you exist.

How is attitude linked to motivation?

People feel more motivated when they are adding value in some way. When you leave people feeling good, you're adding value, and (even if it's unconscious) you feel more motivated about life in general. If you have a negative attitude about everything, people will have a negative picture about you and want to avoid you. You know this unconsciously and feel de-motivated about life as a result.

How does your own bad attitude affect you?

How much peace of mind do cynics have? How many friends do they have? How motivated are they? You'll feel unhappy, bitter, resentful, and frustrated if your attitude is negative.

When do you need an attitude revamp?

Your life will tell you. If things aren't going well, perhaps you need a change of attitude. It's not always easy to change your attitude if life has been handing you tough times. Still, there are always some benefits to these hard times. Focus on what is right and working. Remember that there is good and bad in everyone's life. Look for the good to appreciate life and don't let the bad take over your attitude.

A bad attitude can be fixed. If you think about your successes, attitude is not everything, but it certainly plays a large role. Consider the following two scenarios:

Scenario 1: Your boss walks into the office and says he has an important job for you. You sigh. Your shoulders slump. You think, "Why has be picked on me?" You groan as you think about the fact that you don't have all the knowledge you need. You procrastinate. You do a half-hearted job and hand it in late.

Scenario 2: Your boss walks into the office, talks to the guy in the cubicle next door, and says he has an important job for him. He jumps up, shoulders straight and says, "Bring it on!" (You think he's such a jerk!) He doesn't have the knowledge to do the job, so immediately starts doing some research. He asks for help. He does the best he can do and gets the job in on time.

Scenario 1: When you arrive in the mornings, you feel grumpy. You catch someone in the coffee room and pour out all the reasons you wish you were elsewhere. You slink into your seat without greeting anybody. You spend an hour on Facebook and then reply to your personal emails.

Scenario 2: The guy next door bounds in every morning, smiles at people and asks how they're doing. He gets going on his important projects and leaves Facebook for his lunch break.

Who do you think will get the better increase and a promotion when it's due?

Who do you think feels more motivated about life?

Ok, admittedly this example is grossly exaggerated to illustrate the point. But it's true that a good attitude gets you the promotion. If you were in the position to choose one of the guys above to promote, who would that be? I'm not encouraging you to suck up to your boss and be a "yes" man. What I'm suggesting it that you look at how your attitude affects those around you – and take in the impact that this has on your life.

Did you ever experiment with a tuning fork at school? If you hold a tuning fork in each hand and rap one against a hard surface, what do you see? It starts vibrating and ringing. Now if you move that fork towards the tuning fork in your other hand (don't let them touch) you will notice how the second tuning fork begins vibrating and ringing too. This is called resonance.

Resonance works with people too!

You may be aware of how other people have an influence over your mental state. Moaning, negative, complaining people may leave you feeling grumpy. When you are in the company of an enthusiastic, upbeat person, the chances are that you'll leave their company feeling good. You are attracted to people who demonstrate a healthy mental attitude. And you'll notice that these people have more friends and are healthier overall. Your attitudes, actions and thoughts may be influenced by other people's attitudes and thoughts. Of course, the more aware you are of your own thoughts and feelings, the more control you have over the influence of others on your own mental state.

This is all very well. On the flip side: how are your thoughts and attitudes influencing others?

When people are negatively affected by your attitude, they want to spend less time in your company. They also have a bleak picture of you in their minds. When people feel good after being in your company, they naturally want to spend more time with you. They also have a constructive picture of you in their heads. This is also true of people very close to you. Think about your family. How do they feel when they walk out the door in the morning? How do they feel when they go to bed after spending a few hours with you?

While you are NOT responsible for the thoughts and attitudes of others, you certainly can have an INFLUENCE over them – that's what resonance is all about! You are, however, responsible for your OWN thoughts and actions, and these have an impact on the people around you. The greatest gift you can give to others is to ensure that your tuning fork is vibrating in a way that improves the mental state of others. You don't have to do this, of course. Be aware, though, that your influence on the world around you can either be constructive OR destructive — the choice is yours. The universe tends to reflect back at you what you put into life anyway.

Journal work

Think about an area of your life that's not working.

Describe your attitude towards life in this area. What would the right mental attitude be for you to achieve success in this area?

Describe in detail. What small steps can you take today to begin changing this?

How can attitude be changed?

Attitude changes when your perceptions change. A person with a negative mental attitude probably believes things like:

I'm useless.
I'm worthless.
I'll never be a success.
People don't like me.

If you believe that people don't like you, it will affect your attitude towards them: you may not trust them; you're unlikely to be friendly and certainly won't be too willing to open up. People who have this view will have a picture in their mind of you – that you're unfriendly and withdrawn. When they interact with you, they're reacting to their internal picture of you (not the real you!). So, you can see that this belief does not serve you well in life because if affects every interaction you have with people. It would be very useful to drop that belief and adapt a more empowering belief like, "People appreciate me."

Journal work

Think about a goal of yours that you've never been able to achieve. (Choose something realistic that in theory you should have been able to do). Answer these questions in your journal:

What's stopping me from achieving this goal?

Where did this belief come from?

Who gave me this belief?

How do I feel about that person? Do I regard them highly and respect them?

What does this belief do for me?

What is this belief costing me?

How will my life be different if I let go of this limiting belief?

What concrete evidence do I have to support this belief?

What is the positive intention behind keeping this limiting belief? (This belief is trying to do something good for you in its own way – what is that?)

How else can I satisfy this positive intention without relying on this limiting belief?

Once you have identified some limiting beliefs, you can begin to work on changing them and thus renewing your mental attitude.

Journal work

Answer these questions fully in your journal:

How well is my present attitude serving me? (Am I getting what I want?)

Am I happy with the response I get from people?

What do I believe about myself? How can I prove this to myself?

What are my expectations about what life offers me?

Where do I need to make changes?

What resources are available to help me make changes to my attitude?

What three beliefs could I adopt to help develop the right attitude?

Cultivate new beliefs to support the right mental attitude. These may include:

I have the resources to achieve success.
I can!
I see what's right and good and will build on this.

Once you've decided on a new belief, you need to make it stick. Think of your belief like a table. You need to give the table four legs so that it is strong and stable. You give this belief legs by finding four behaviors that support it. It's a little upside down, but it works! If you sincerely believed this statement, how would your behaviour be different? Adopt these four behaviors and stick to them for a month — the belief will become embedded in your unconscious.

For instance: let's say you want to believe the thought, "I have the resources to achieve success." If you really believed you had all the resources you needed, how would you behave?

The first thing I would do each day is an important task that'll help me reach my goal.

I'd only spend one hour a day on emails.

If I need something from someone, I'd ask them for it.

I'd focus on the next step.

Go ahead and religiously adopt these behaviors for a month. You'll be amazed at the successes you can notch up in one month with these actions! Repeat for a few months, enjoy your successes for a few months and you will KNOW that you have what it takes.

Practice

Choose a new belief that will support you in getting what you want in life. Decide on four behaviors you can adopt that would validate this belief.

Make sure the behaviors are small things that can be executed every day. Use technology (like reminders on your phone or email) to remind you to do these four tasks daily.

Repeat for 30 days. If you skip a day or two, don't give up. Start again and repeat for 30 days.

There's not a single part of your life that is not affected by your attitude. Your future will definitely be influenced by the attitude you carry with you.

If you want to read more on attitude, check out my book, Change Your Attitude, Change Your Life

Journal work

Think about your diary for the next week. Identify an interaction that you'll be having with someone – business or personal.

When this interaction is complete, in what sort of mental state would you like to leave the other person?

What mental attitude to this person will work best?

What can you give to this interaction that will help you leave the person in the desired mental state?

What mental state would you like to be in after the interaction?

What do you need to bring to the meeting to achieve this?

Chapter 6: Where Are You Going?

Journal work

First, spend five minutes reflecting on your life. Consider all aspects: your way of being in the world; your work; your relationships; your leisure time; your passions; your successes and failures. Now write a paragraph of about 400 words that concisely answers this question: Where are you now?

Picture this: you wake up to the alarm. You stretch leisurely, smile to yourself and jump out of bed. The cold tiles shock your feet slightly. As you shower, you briefly consider the journey ahead. You dress quickly. You glance in the mirror – as always the sight of you in your uniform gives you a thrill. On the way to your workplace, you focus on calming and grounding yourself and your emotions. It's a big day ahead. When you arrive, you are comforted by the buzz and focused energy of the hundreds of people you see. You slip efficiently through the staff entrance. At your locker, you carefully read all the reports and nod your head in satisfaction — all is ready. The long corridors take you to the small room where you'll be spending the next few hours. You go through the standard checks with focused determination. A uniformed smile opens the door and announces that all 300 of them are present and accounted for and the plane is ready for take-off. You turn to your co-pilot and ask, "Where shall we go today?"

Fortunately this doesn't happen in reality. A pilot has a detailed flight plan and knows exactly where to go. In the same way, you are the pilot of your life. Are you efficiently steering yourself closer to your destination? Are you enjoying the journey?

Are you a "Make it happen" person or a "Wonder what happened?" person?

There is no law against sitting back and seeing where life takes you and certainly this is a valid choice every now and again. However, this way of being in the world dis-empowers you. You're at the mercy of life's whims. I'm wondering how motivated you'll feel if you're not sure where you're going and what life will throw at you next. It's difficult to muster up enthusiasm for something unknown.

You may argue that life will throw things at you anyway. Yes, I agree. However, if you have a plan for your life you may handle these interruptions more easily and can probably learn from them. Like the pilot following a flight plan, life can still throw you off track. Like the pilot following a flight plan, you may have to make some adjustments and get back on track. When you have a plan for your life, you wake up in the mornings with a purpose. You know where you're headed. Motivation and enthusiasm lighten your journey. You feel (mostly) in control and you head out there with determination and focus.

Journal work

Think about a time when you chose a project to do and you completed it successfully. Maybe it was organizing a special holiday or, redecorating a room in your house or, a special project at work. Write about your experiences as you planned the project – how did it feel? What did you think about? How were your motivation levels? How did you handle it when your motivation dipped?

Once the project was wrapped up, what did you experience? How did it feel to complete it? What are your memories of the wrap-up? How has this completed project affected your motivation for other projects? What does this success say about you as a person?

There are three essential steps in executing any plan.

Daydream. Those ideas have to come from somewhere! Allow yourself to daydream and imagine exciting possibilities. Do this often!

Decide. At some stage make a decision – I'm now going to work towards creating this project.

Do. A daydream without action remains a daydream. Once you have decided on a project or destination, take three or four small steps every single day. Take these actions first before you start on your other tasks. That's exactly how I am getting this book written. Believe me, if I left it till after the other work was done, it would never happen. Small steps every day will get you to where you want to go.

While you're taking daily action, refine your daydreams. Every morning, before you crawl (or hop) out of bed, run a movie through your mind of your completed project. How will your life be once it's finished? What will you be seeing and feeling every day? Add colour, sounds and textures to your movie. Make it exciting so that your passion, determination and motivation uplift you as you work on this plan. This is called visualizing.

Visualization is a powerful tool! This technique really works. The wonderful thing is that you already know how to do it – all it takes is using your imagination.

Your imagination is something that you use daily already. What do think is going on when you travel to work every day? Your mind is busy imagining things. You imagine things in the future, like how the meeting will go, or how you will talk to your boss, or how you will make love to your partner. You even imagine things that happened in the past; you might relive that lovemaking, or imagine how you could have handled your boss differently. Yes, you use your imagination all the time. When you visualize, you're using your imagination with purpose. You direct your thoughts just like a movie director.

Let your daydreams open up possibilities for your life. Decide on a project and take action every day. Support yourself through visualization so that passion and motivation live side by side with your dreams. Be like the pilot, following the flight plan, embracing the changes in weather and eventually touching down in the place of your dreams.

Journal work

Imagine that it's two years from now — You wake up; the sun is streaming into your room. You smile and stretch and realize you are living your best life. Describe that life in detail. Have fun with this exercise. Really let go and don't block your imagination in any way. Write freely for about half an hour or until you feel complete. Now close your journal and put it away for a week.

Practice:

Read your journal entry from the previous exercise. Decide to implement a change in your life that takes you one step closer to your best life.

What are the next small steps you can take to begin implementing that change? Take them.

Repeat this daily until that change is integrated in your life.

Your attitude towards failure can make or break your success. If you allow failure to de-motivate you and you decide to give up, success will not be yours.

If you give up, that's it. It's over. You will never get what you set your heart out to achieve. If you keep trying, you'll get there, even if it takes a lifetime.

What do a baby and Thomas Edison have in common? They both kept on trying till they got it! Thomas Edison made many light bulbs (apparently about 99 attempts) before he finally created one that worked – imagine if he had given up after his first 'failure'? Look at a baby learning to walk – how many times do they fall down before they get it right? Imagine if the baby never tried again after the first fall.

Never, Ever Give Up!

One of the greatest stumbling blocks to your success is the fear of failure. If you're avoiding taking action because you're afraid that you might fail, you're limiting your life hugely. Through life's ups and downs, somehow you learned to fear failure. You beat yourself up whenever you make a mistake. At school you got big red marks scribbled across 'bad' tests. At school you either failed, or you passed. Did anyone ask you what you learned in the process of 'failing'? Did anyone ask you what you can do differently in the future? Did anyone offer to support you in going forward? Probably not. If you failed, you got into trouble and that was that. It's no wonder that so many people have developed a fear of failure.

These fears are often carried into the workplace where your success is measured by your performance on the last project. One of the best ways of finding out how you are doing is to ask for feedback from your colleagues or boss (or even your spouse). Very often, you don't ask for feedback because you're terrified that it may be negative.

If you were able to get this feedback, you would be able to adjust your actions, do something differently so that you can improve on it. By not asking for feedback, you are missing out on crucial learning.

You may also have difficulty forgiving yourself when you get it wrong. If you fail, you might want to hide your failure and never try again. What happened? You started seeing mistakes or problems as bad – instead of feeling excited about the fact that you've just learned something of value.

Failure is merely feedback. It's the universe's way of telling us that something you are doing doesn't work. The important thing IS TO LEARN! See failure (or feedback) as a necessary part of your development. Generally, if you look at the feedback (failure) you're getting from life, and you adjust your actions so that you do it differently in the future, then you've made progress. And, if you are progressing, I would call that being a success. A wise person keeps making different mistakes. A fool keeps repeating the same mistakes. If it doesn't work – don't do it again.

As you move through life, achieving goals and successes, you build up a repertoire of things that work and things that don't. How wonderful!

Journal work

Write down all the failure you've experienced in the last few years including big ones and small ones. Then, answer the following questions fully:

What role did I play in each of these failures?

What did I learn from each of these failures?

What will I do differently in the future?

What opportunities am I saying no to at this present time?

In what ways am I limiting myself by saying no to these opportunities?

What will I do differently?

If you are saying no, or avoiding things because you're afraid of failure, look at how you are limiting your life. Remember that failure is never permanent. It's a moment in time. Change your perception of failure. Change your attitude to failure. Change your thinking about failure. When something goes wrong, look for the reasons.

Explore and learn. Then do it again – with your newly acquired knowledge – and do it differently. Make your 'failures' work for you. The very worst thing that can happen if you fail is that you will learn something that can move you closer to success. What have you got to lose?

Never, ever give up!

Practice
 Every day this week, talk to yourself out loud! Remind yourself that failure is merely feedback. Say it a few times. Then have a debate with yourself where you prove the statement. Find some examples that happened to you recently.

Conclusion

The biggest distraction for me is my email. For others it is social media. This morning I decided not to open my email or look at Facebook until I had written for two hours. I wasn't in the mood for writing – it had been a hectic week. Part of me wants to rest – after all, I've had a hard week. Another part of me is nagging because I want to get this book completed. I also know that if I start checking my mail an hour can disappear before I know it. So that's what I did. I ignored my email and sat down and started writing. After a few minutes, the conflicting parts of me grew quiet and I started enjoying myself.

What I do know is this: even if you are motivated to achieve something, there will be moments on the journey when you just don't feel like doing the work. At these times, acknowledge that you don't feel like it and start the work anyway. The motivation will flow back while you are busy.

This book shows you many ways to improve your motivation. There are tricks and tools. A self-reflective journey is also on offer. Take what you need from the book. Keep those things in your own special toolkit. Use them whenever necessary. You will find that the more you use them, the easier it will be to get started and get going. Once you're going, you'll relax into the work and enjoy the process. As Gary Player said, "The more I practice, the luckier I get." So will you.

It's amazing what you can achieve when you're motivated. Remember the last time you were really motivated about something? You did it without having to push yourself too much. Procrastination did not come into the picture. You did the work because you wanted to and you were excited about the outcome. That's the magic of motivation.

About the Author

I'm Dr. Marybeth Crane. I hope you enjoyed this component of my holistic wellness series of short reads. Wellness encompasses not only your physical and mental health, but also your spiritual health and financial health. My main goal in sharing with you my wellness series is to help you attain a happy, healthy life and make age just a number!

I'm a board-certified Podiatric foot and ankle surgeon who has been in private practice, specializing in sports medicine, for over 25 years. I have built a multi-million-dollar private practice and lecture often on business and practice management topics.

I have written several books on running injuries and author a blog at www.myrundoc.com that is solely focused on sports medicine and running topics. I also author a blog on women's health and wellness issues as well as relationships, communication and the issues surrounding the lovely aging process at www.fitfiftyandfabulous.com.

My goal as a motivational speaker is to convince everyone that positive thinking is potent, exercise is the most powerful drug we as physicians can prescribe and choosing a healthy lifestyle will help combat the lovely aging process. I can help you with the small and big changes that will assist you in changing your life for the better! The one percent changes daily are mighty!

In my spare time, I have been competitively running for more than 40 years. It definitely helps burn off the crazy! I have completed more than 20 marathons, a dozen or so Half-Ironman and 2 Full Ironman Triathlons. I have three wonderful daughters and two stepdaughters; so, we also have a boy dog! My husband is truly a saint.

Contact me at marybeth@fitfiftyandfabulous.com. Follow me @myrundoc on Twitter, @fitfiftyandfabulous on Facebook, and @myrundoc.crane on Instagram. I look forward to your questions and comments.

If Your Running Feet Could Talk
Change Your Attitude, Change Your Life: The Power of Optimism
Stress Relief Meditation
The Money Cleanse
Stop Procrastinating: How to Get Your Sh*t Done!
Stop Overdrinking: Rethinking Your Relationship with Alcohol
Self-Motivation: How to Get Motivated, Stay Motivated and Live
Motivated
Coming Soon: Finding Your Purpose

www.ingramcontent.com/pod-product-compliance
Lightning Source LLC
Chambersburg PA
CBHW030526220526
45463CB00007B/2733